LOVE'S FIRE

by the same author

poetry

WINTER SCARECROW
MASKS AND FACES
EVIDENCE
HOMAGE TO TOUKARAM
THE FABIUS POEMS
A FULL CIRCLE
NO DIAMONDS, NO HAT, NO HONEY

translations
(with Anne Pennington)

MACEDONIAN SONGS
BLAZHE KONESKY (SELECTED POEMS)
THE GOLDEN APPLE

fiction

ONE LAST MIRROR
BURNING HOUSES
THE WEB

non-fiction

A JOURNEY IN LADAKH

LOVE'S FIRE

RE-CREATIONS OF RUMI

Andrew Harvey

Meeramma
Ithaca, New York USA

Meeramma Publications
26 Spruce Lane
Ithaca, New York 14850
USA

Printed in USA

ISBN: 0-9622973-0-5

Library of Congress Cataloging-in-Publication Data

Jalāl al-Dīn Rūmī, Maulana, 1207-1273.
   Love's fire.

   "The great majority of these 're-creations' of Rūmī
are taken from his Rubaiyat"—Pref.
   1. Sufi poetry, Persian—Translations into English.
2. English poetry—Translations from Persian. I. Harvey,
Andrew, 1952-   . II. Jalāl al-Dīn Rūmī, Maulana,
1207-1273. Rubā ⁵īyāt. English. Selections. 1989.
II. Title.
PK6480.E5H37   1989   891'.5511   89-12305
ISBN 0-9622973-0-5

for Mother Meera

Preface

The great majority of these 're-creations' of Rumi are taken from his Rubaiyat, a collection of quatrains in classical Persian; the rest are taken from other sources in his work. They are mostly poems of mystic passion and illumination inspired by his Master, Shams I Tabriz. Rumi met Shams in Konya, Southern Turkey, in 1244, when he was about thirty-five years old, a respected intellectual with a tidy life. Shams shattered that life with the power and fury of his spiritual presence and transformed the theologian into an ecstatic. In 1247 Shams disappeared (he may even have been murdered by some of Rumi's pupils). Rumi was stricken, but his grief and the memory of the ecstasy Shams had given him made him a great mystic poet. From his despair at his Master's absence, he fashioned poems that enshrine and celebrate the mystery of a Presence beyond time or space. Rumi spent the last period of his life as a Master in his own right, speaking of Shams as of his Self and of his love for Shams as indistinguishable from his love of God. These poems arise from this vast love and the awareness that was born from its fire. Rumi paid an extreme price for gnosis, as perhaps all mystics must be prepared to, but the gratitude and sense of glory that irradiate even his poems of terror and self-annihilation show that he knew it was worth everything.

There are 108 poems in this book because 108 is the sacred number of the East and the number of beads on a mala (rosary). I have arranged them to represent and enact the drama of longing, fulfillment, loss, mourning and final Union that Rumi lived through. They should be read separately and then together as part of one long Passion Play of the soul.

Over the five years that I have been working on these versions, I have consulted many Persian scholars, Sufis of various nationalities, translations, glosses, and critical works in German, French, Italian and Spanish. I have myself lived through 'a process' with a Master. This work is dedicated to Her.

Rumi wrote a densely woven Persian; sometimes I have had to sacrifice allusiveness for immediacy. On rare occasions I have slightly expanded or condensed a poem.

Andrew Harvey
Thalheim, March 1988

'Love is that flame that, when it is kindled, burns everything away; God only remains.'

RUMI, *Discourses*

What do you hope to find
In the soul's streets
In the bloody streets of the heart
That have no news, even of yourself?

Anywhere you find a lullaby
Leave; safety's final danger.
When you come across a story-teller—
Know a house is being destroyed.

Never think the earth void or dead—
It's a hare, awake with shut eyes:
It's a sauce-pan, simmering with broth—
One clear look, you'll see it's in ferment.

Ignorant men are the soul's enemy
Shatter the jar of smug words
Cling for life to those who know
Prop a mirror in water, it rusts

How long will we fill our pockets
Like children with dirt and stones?
Let the world go. Holding it
We never know ourselves, never are air-born.

I lost my world, my fame, my mind—
The Sun appeared, and all the shadows ran.
I ran after them, but vanished as I ran—
Light ran after me and hunted me down.

Circle the Sun, you become a sun:
Circle a Master, and you become one.
You'd be a ruby, if you danced round this mine—
Dance round him, you'll glitter like gold.

This body's a mirror of heaven:
Its energies make angels jealous.
Our purity astounds seraphim:
Devils shiver at our nerve.

Body of earth, don't talk of earth
Tell the story of pure mirrors
The Creator has given you this splendour—
Why talk of anything else?

Suddenly, he is here—
Heads touch, secrets start singing.
Time's barn is flattened by storm-wind
We crumple on its straw like drunks.

No-one can wear the jewel of reality
Except the One in whose fire it was born.
I have a friend who wears it on his forehead—
Our foreheads touch tonight, and mine burns.

In love with him, my soul
Lives the subtlest of passions
Lives like a gypsy—
Each day a different house
Each night under the stars.

I was once, like you, 'enlightened,' 'rational,'
I too scoffed at lovers.
Now I am drunk, crazed, thin with misery—
No-one's safe! Watch out!

Atom, you want to flee the sun?
Madman, give up!
You're a jar; fate's a stone—
Kick against it, you'll waste your wine.

Reason, leave now! You'll not find wisdom here!
Were you thin as a hair, there'd still be no room.
The Sun is risen! In its vast dazzle
Every lamp is drowned.

Over all the parchments of Egypt
I've scrawled my cries and hungers.
One hour of love's worth a hundred worlds—
I've thousands of hearts; here, burn them all.

Desperation, let me always know
How to welcome you—
And put in your hands the torch
To burn down the house.

Light the incense!
You have to burn to be fragrant.
To scent the whole house
You have to burn to the ground.

You only need smell the wine
For vision to flame from each void—
Such flames from wine's aroma!
Imagine if you were the wine.

The thread of your love is thin
Far sharper than any knife
Wind it round my mind
Pull it, until I end

There's always another death to die
Beyond the death you know
Always another door of scars
To open to another room.

One look from you, and I look
At you in all things
Looking back at me; those eyes
In which all things live and burn.

In the driest whitest stretch
Of pain's infinite desert
I lost my sanity
And found this rose.

I am so close to you I am distant
I am so mingled with you I am apart
I am so open I am hidden
I am so stong I totter

You see through each cloak I wear
Know if I speak without mouth or language.
The world is drunk on its desire for words:
I am the slave of the Master of silence.

Keep my mysteries in your soul's treasure-chest:
Dissimulate my ecstasies even to yourself.
If you find me, hide me in your heart:
Know my madness as absolute truth.

I shout 'I'm my own man'
Then 'I'm my own victim'
Smart banal games! Love, help me
Choose not to choose.

I can't know, only you can,
What makes my heart laugh,
This branch of flowers
Shaking in your wind.

You're sea; I'm fish.
You're desert; I'm gazelle.
Fill me with your breath, I live on it,
I'm your reed, your reed.

'You're the soul,' I said, 'You can't leave the body.'
'How can you know the soul,' he said, 'as you know the
    body?'
'You're the sea of goodness,' I said. 'Silence!' he said
'Love's a jewel you can't hand over like a stone.'

Heart, if you can't brave grief, go—
Love's glory's not a small thing.
Soul, come in, if you're fearless:
Shudder, and this is not your house.

When my eyes are blind, what use is collyrium?
When my heart's in fragments, what use fidelity?
When soul and heart are ash from longing for you
What use are your seductive words?

Have you no dignity, my heart
Scattering always like dust in wind?
You're in the fire? Let's leave you there—
Terror will make you subtle.

Near truth's blaze what are 'doubt' or 'certainty'?
Bitterness dies near the honey of truth.
Doesn't the sun hide its face before his?
What are these small lights that linger?

All the world's passions are simple
Beside this passion; cool beside this
Fire I am in that ignites the world
And shall destroy it.

I groaned, he burnt me while I groaned
I fell silent, his fire fell on me
He drove me out beyond all limit
I ran inside, he burnt me there

I groaned; 'Be quiet,' he said.
I was quiet: he said, 'Groan!'
I grew feverish: he said, 'Be calm!'
I grew calm; he said, 'I want you to burn.'

Pain is the wind his flags unfurl in
The desert his stallions cross and re-cross
Without check or end—
He is my anguish and I am his.

Hold to what can never be held
So your hands become ghosts:
His hands are clear spirit
How could they hold bone?

If I'd known how savage Love is
I'd have blocked the door of Love's house
Beaten a drum, shouted 'Keep away!'
But I'm in the house...helpless...

'No-one suffers enough,' he said, 'Be the one
Who suffers everything and comes to me
With nothing but this bowl
Into which I can pour my wine.'

Love's day hasn't yet come.
I should retreat from Love a little...
My heart cries 'That's impossible!'
Bows its head, smiles to itself.

Loving you, I've lost all friends, all enemies
Neither 'cup' nor 'jar' remain.
You've drunk my blood!
I smell it on your lips.

I do nothing any more but suffer for you,
Sow in ruin the seed of passion:
Sculpt, day and night, the face of union:
Spirit the hammer, anguish the stone.

Pain is the cradle of Vision
Death the mother that rocks it. . .
'This is the Law,' he said quietly.
'Drink my wine, and dance.'

He arrived suddenly, drunk,
Sat down, downed cup after cup. . .
Drinking in his curls of fire
Made my face eyes, my eyes hands.

Tell the night 'Our day has no night
Our religion no law but love
Love is this shoreless sea
We drown in saying not a word'

I call you and screens fall between us
Your face's dazzle shrouds your face:
Saying 'your lips' robs me of them . . .
Silence! Talk strangles love!

Still talking, still talking. . .
Even as night floods our bed.
Keep pouring the wine
I long to lose my head.

Today, you pulled me to you secretly
I grew wild, broke my last chains.
I am thousands of drunks together, not just one,
Mad, in love with all madmen.

White flame
On a day without wind
My love is burning
Away my mind

Ghostly passions are the most violent.
No-one who does not know this can know
Why I lie down in his desert
For his stallions to trample.

You are the moon: I am your face in a pool.
How could I forget that night you said,
Holding my head, 'I am yours always
Your love came from me; I am your soul.'

Of my bones he made the flutes of heaven
And of my skin dried for years
In the wind of longing
This parchment on which he brands his sign.

He's fire
I'm oil
This smoke you see around him
Is me
.

Lift the veils tonight, lift them all.
Don't leave one thread hanging. . .
Yesterday you were talking about 'soul' and 'heart'—
Here they are before you, charred and bleeding.

Tonight is the night; sad; radiant;
When our mysteries are fulfilled.
All my mysteries are images of you—
Night, be long! He and I are lost in love.

'You could have had anything,' you once said.
I laughed. What could anything be
Without you? All the world is driftwood
Thrown up from your sea.

Yesterday he gazed at me, and said
'Without me, how will you live?'
'Like a fish on burning sand.'
'You are to blame,' he said, and wept.

Bitter the years without him
Bitter the years with him
But the second bitterness
Tastes of burning suns.

'When you think of me' you said
'Do not think of me:
Clear the house of everything
So it holds nothing but sun.'

Once you said 'I cannot leave
Anyone who's loved me'
Your disappearance
Remains

Sunlight in a filthy street
His absence ringing in my ears
Nothing to show for a lifetime's love
But this broken bowl, these tears.

This heart I believed mine for so long
I can't just 'leave' it, even with friends.
My lover has left me and gone near you—
Keep safe what I kept with so many tears.

I live in terror of not dying
Of never being him and always me
This carcass whose works are coins
Rattling in a beggar's tin.

Heart, be grave now; bear your grief.
The soul will be your slave if you bear grief.
The world's wealth is yours if you have courage,
If you drink your dark palmful from love's hand.

Grieve for him all your life
Make life your grief for him:
Grief with its hidden smile
Transparent as a twig in April.

He is in each of my atoms,
Each of my raw nerves. . .
I'm a harp leaning against him
This grief just a play of his fingers.

At the end of pain
A quiet white exhaustion
Your ghost sits down in
To take my head in its hands.

When I am sad, I am radiant
When I am broken, content
When I am tranquil and silent as the earth
My cries like thunder tremble heaven.

All I know is I know nothing—
And knowing that is by his grace.
I dance in the dirt outside his house.
I gaze up at the window lit with him.

Everything I am
I draw from you
Battered old bucket
Dipping in your well.

For you; this language without words
Kept secret from all other ears. . .
Only you hear what I say
Even when I'm shouting in a crowd.

How open we were that day, tender and delicious,
No longer bodies at all; pure soul.
I'm afraid and alone—give me a sign;
Make us again as you made us then.

This mystery; I hear your voice and find mine
Boundless like the grace of God.
You've caught me a hundred times—
Catch me again, now; make me new.

Take my soul, now. Send me reeling
Drunkenly out of the world...
Everything in me good, but not you—
Destroy. Turn this wood to fire.

It is he who suffers his absence in me
Who through me cries out to himself.
Love's most strange, most holy mystery—
We are intimate beyond belief.

I know nothing any more, except
That knowing you, I know the source
Of Knowing; this fire-spring you pull me in
Sometimes, where 'you' and 'I' burn.

He is here, who was never gone
The water never left this river
He is pure musk, I his scent
Can you smell one without the other?

I'm a mountain; his voice is this echo
I'm a painting; his brush is always changing me
I'm a lock creaking as his key turns—
You still believe these words are 'mine'?

How many times must I say it?
The madman of reason is the man of wisdom
Follow grief's road to the heart
You'll find in your self thousands of strangers.

These atoms whirling through the world
Are nothing but madmen!
Can't you see them dancing
Lost, dazzled, in him?

Each atom, each image, is a seer and a prophet
Alive, on fire, with our pain and love.
Open your eyes! Make your life an ear!
The news must go on and on arriving.

I am soul with a hundred thousand bodies
Yet there's no 'soul' or 'body'; the two are myself.
I've played a strange game, changed into another;
This new myself's more beautiful, and wilder.

One day in your wineshop I drank a little wine
And threw off the robe of this body:
I knew, drunk on you, this world is harmony—
Creation, destruction, I'm dancing for them both.

Spring's fire-birds are in the trees!
The crow's noose is ash!
I want, like the lily and rose,
To peel myself of myself,
Run, like melting snow-water,
From garden to garden.

Soul with a hundred thousand bodies
Everything's myself; I talk only of me.
Like a wave I rise in my own body—
Sea and wave the same wild water.

What passed between us yesterday
Could never be written or said.
The day I leave this ruined country
You'll read it in the folds of my shroud.

I am doubt, faith, passion, purity,
Old-man, young-man, sage and baby.
Don't say when I die 'He's dead'
I'll be living at last, alive in love.

'Come to the spring garden,' they said,
'Its air is song; you can't hear the crow.'
In my soul there lives a marvellous painter
Who paints on each crow-feather a thousand
    gardens.

I burn away; laugh; my ashes are alive!
I die a thousand times:
My ashes dance back—
A thousand new faces.

Cloud pregnant with a million bolts of lightning
Love gives birth to the philosopher's stone.
My soul is flooded by your sea of splendour
Being and Cosmos drown there silently.

On the Day of Resurrection men will stagger
Before you pale and trembling with terror:
I will hold up your love to you and say
'Ask it anything; it speaks for me.'

Now I know that love is with me always
His soft and fiery curls always in my hand:
However drunk the wine made me yesterday
Today his wine is drunk in me.

You were in me; I brewed with ecstasy
Whipped like a sea by my own winds.
Shaken out in thunder, I told the sea's secrets
Slept in clouds along the shore.

In the end I shall be at an end
Nothing but grief and love
Mixed in a dark transparent wine
You down in one gulp.

To die in life is to become life.
The wind stops skirting you
And enters. All the roses, suddenly,
Are blooming in your skull.

You are the hidden king of the heart
Our soul's healer, magician of being—
When your rain falls, we gather in your garden
When it rains, we dance.

The soul's extravagance is endless:
Spring after spring after spring. . .
We are your gardens dying, blossoming.

Don't call him 'this' or 'that'
In the love I know what word could stay?
Language is just a handful of dust
A breath of his blows away.

Whatever they say or think—
I am in you and am you.
No-one can understand this
Until he's lost his mind.

After the certainties, the visions—
This final loneliness
You flower in

This isn't spring, it's another season;
A hidden union makes our eyes swim.
All our trees' branches dance in this rain—
Each, for a secret reason.

You've talked so much you've gone beyond words
Circled him so long you've become him:
Driven your boats of words so far into the water
Neither words nor boat remain; nor you.

At an end of 'myself'
He appears
That Face
Through these rags

For days I am no longer
In the world. Nor am I
Out of it. Not 'here', not 'there'—
Silence, light, air.

A horseman flashed by, then vanished
In a whirlwind of dust.
The dust stays. Shines on all things.
This is Eternity's house.

The tender words we said to one another
Are stored in the secret heart of heaven:
One day like rain they will fall and spread,
And our mystery will grow green over the world.